Easy Classical Pian

MW01257649

FOR TEACHER AND STUDENT

Selected and Edited by Gayle Kowalchyk and E. L. Lancaster

ABOUT THIS COLLECTION

The two volumes, *Easy Classical Piano Duets for Teacher and Student,* Books 1 and 2, have been successful with beginning students of all ages. Book 3 was compiled to meet the needs of teachers who want teacher-student duets limited to single five-finger positions utilizing more complex rhythms and more sophisticated articulations. In addition, the duets in this collection are generally longer than the duets in *Easy Classical Piano Duets for Teacher and Student,* Books 1 and 2.

This collection contains teacher-student duets written by eight teachers and composers who lived in the 18th, 19th and 20th centuries. To facilitate ease in reading the score by young students, the primo and secondo are on separate pages. The student parts are limited to a single five-finger position, are notated in treble and bass clef, and fall mostly within the grand-staff reading range.

Arranged in approximate order of difficulty of the student part, the duets can be used for sight reading or ensemble repertoire. Students will be motivated by the full sounds that result from the added teacher part as they acquire security with tempo and rhythm provided by ensemble performance. Enjoy!

Becucci, Ernesto (from *Tre Piccole Ricreazioni*)
Smile, Op. 280, No. 1 6

Diabelli, Anton (from *Melodious Pieces*)
Andante cantabile, Op. 149, No. 18 54

Romanza (Andantino), Op. 149, No. 11 26

(from *Pleasures of Youth*)
Rondo (Allegro), Op. 163, No. 6 50

Emery, Stephen A. (from *Ein Abend zu Hause*)
The Sleepy Boy, Op. 26, No. 6...30

Grimaldi, François (from *Trois Morceaux*)
Mazurka Amusante, Op. 53, No. 2 40

Gurlitt, Cornelius (from *Der Anfänger*)
Dance, Op. 211, No. 17 60

Landry, Albert (from *Illusions*)
The Wooden Horse, Op. 266, No. 1..20

In a Boat, Op. 266, No. 2...12

The Bicycle, Op. 266, No. 3..34

Reinecke, Carl (from *Vierhändige Clavierstücke*)
Allegretto, Op. 54, No. 1 2

Andante, Op. 54, No. 2 28

Rosenauer, Alois (from *Leichte Compositionen*)
Ballade, Op. 26, No. 1..44

(from *Drei Vorspielstücke*)
Barcarole, Op. 17, No. 1 56

About the Composers 64

Copyright © MCMXCIX by Alfred Publishing Co., Inc.
All rights reserved. Printed in USA.

SECONDO
Teacher

Allegretto
from *Vierhändige Clavierstücke*

Carl Reinecke (1824–1910)
Op. 54, No. 1

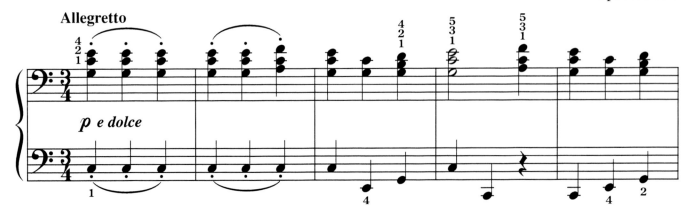

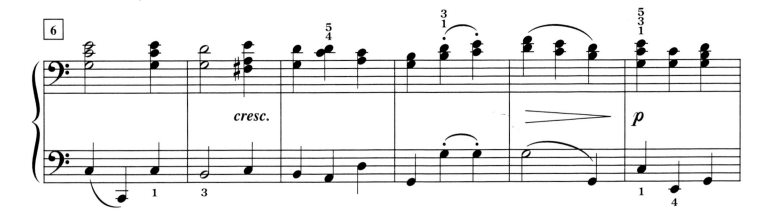

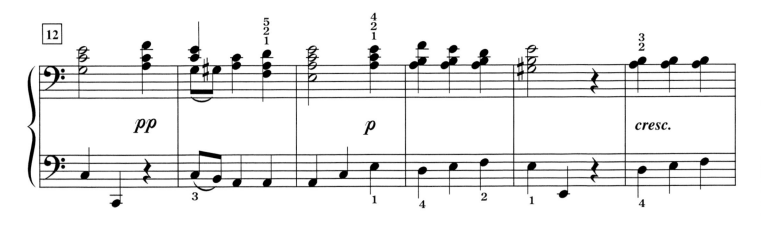

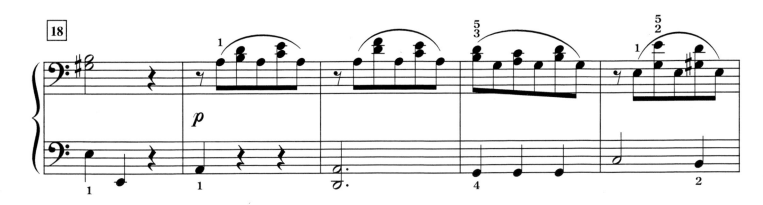

PRIMO
Student

Allegretto
from *Vierhändige Clavierstücke*

Carl Reinecke (1824–1910)
Op. 54, No. 1

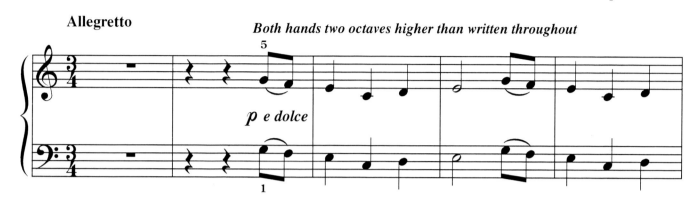

SECONDO (Teacher)

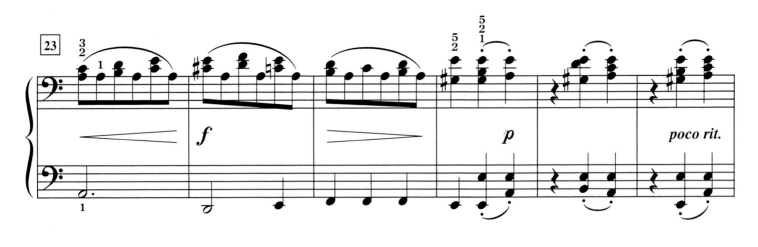

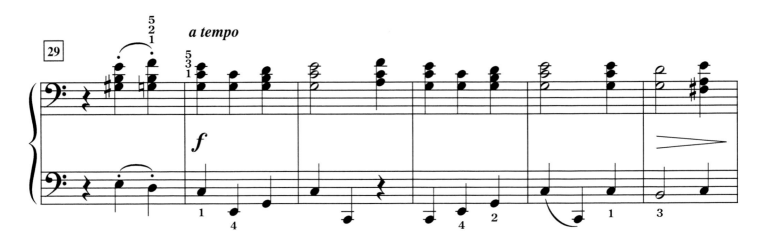

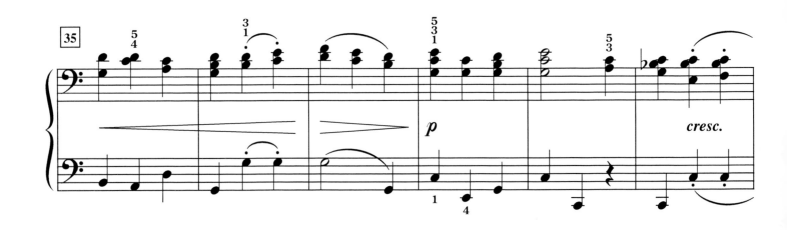

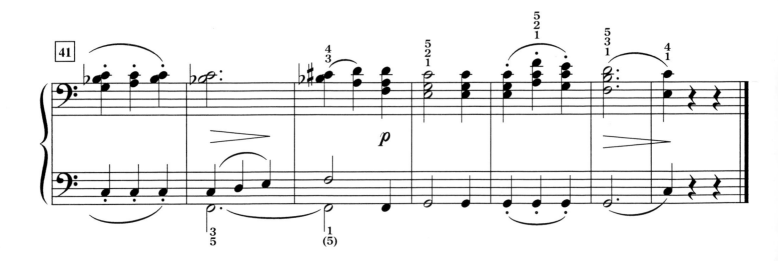

PRIMO (Student)

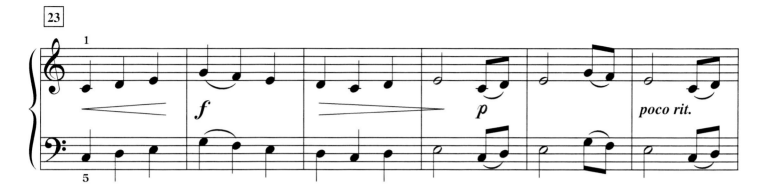

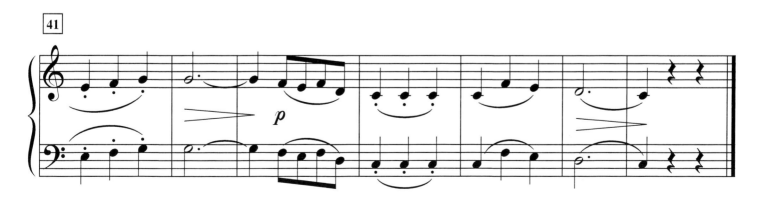

SECONDO
Teacher

Smile
from *Tre Piccole Ricreazioni*

Ernesto Becucci (1845–1905)
Op. 280, No. 1

Tempo di gavotta: moderato

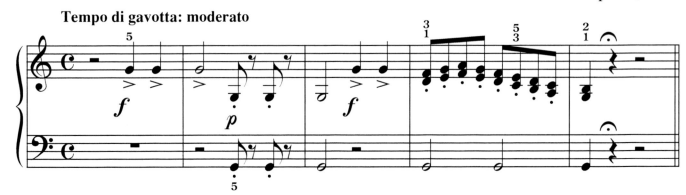

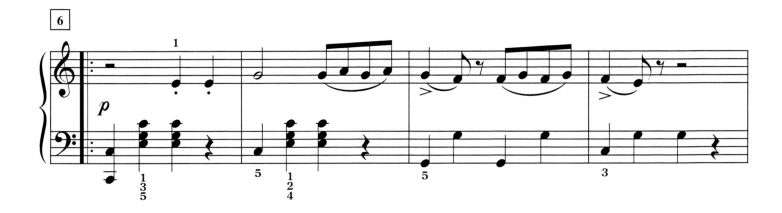

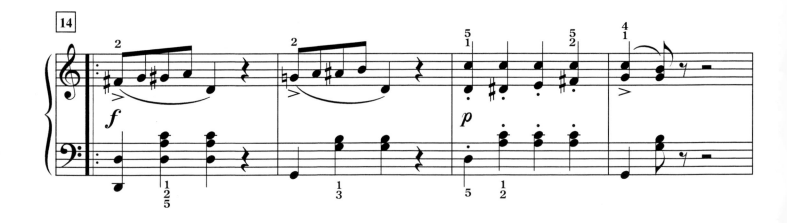

PRIMO
Student

Smile

from *Tre Piccole Ricreazioni*

Ernesto Becucci (1845–1905)

Op. 280, No. 1

Tempo di gavotta: moderato

Both hands two octaves higher than written throughout

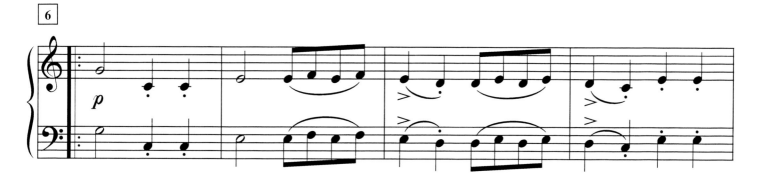

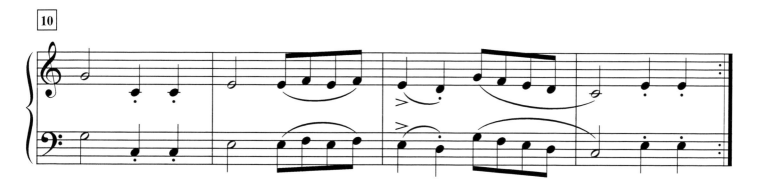

SECONDO (Teacher)

PRIMO (Student)

SECONDO (Teacher)

SECONDO
Teacher

In a Boat
from *Illusions*

Albert Landry (dates unknown)
Op. 266, No. 2

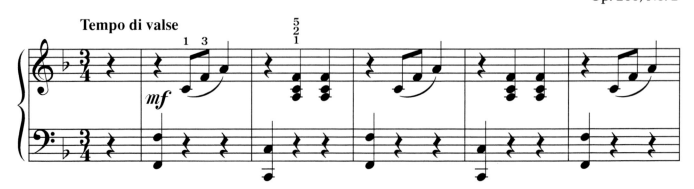

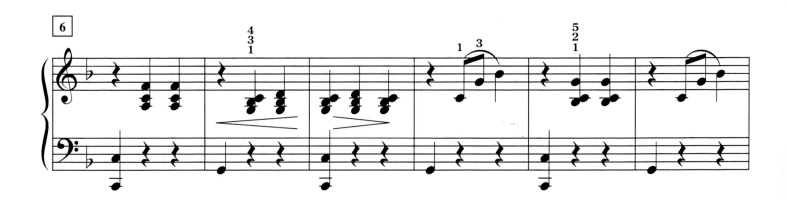

PRIMO
Student

In a Boat
from *Illusions*

Albert Landry (dates unknown)
Op. 266, No. 2

Tempo di valse
Both hands two octaves higher than written throughout

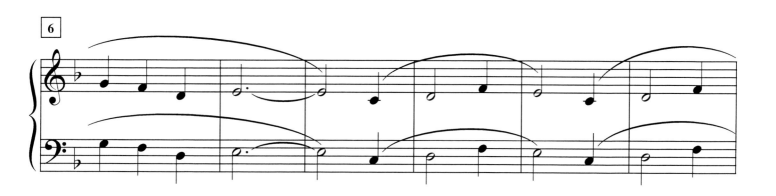

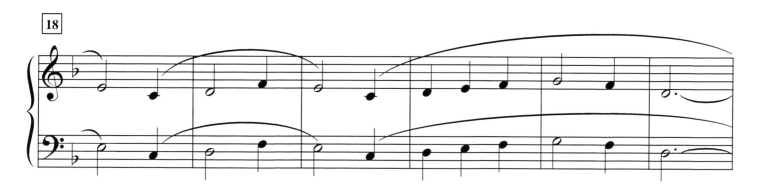

SECONDO (Teacher)

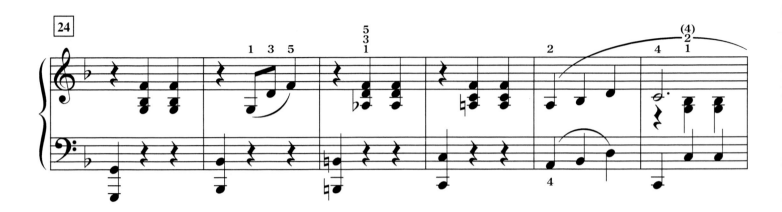

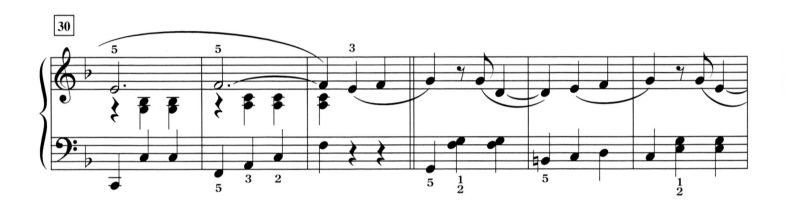

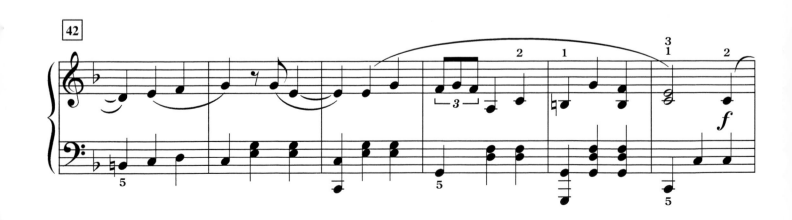

PRIMO (Student)

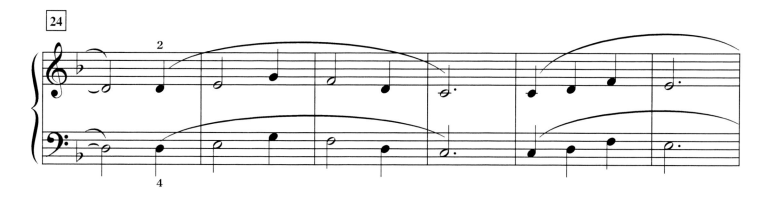

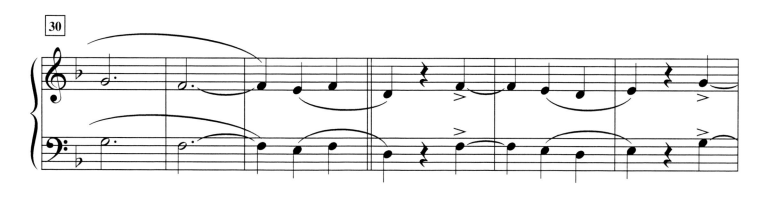

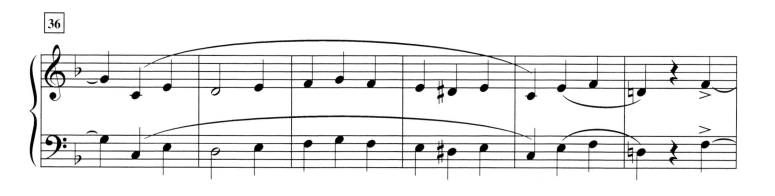

SECONDO (Teacher)

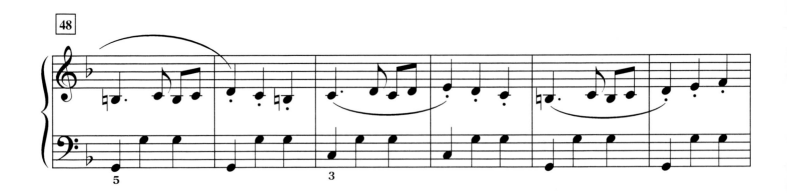

PRIMO (Student)

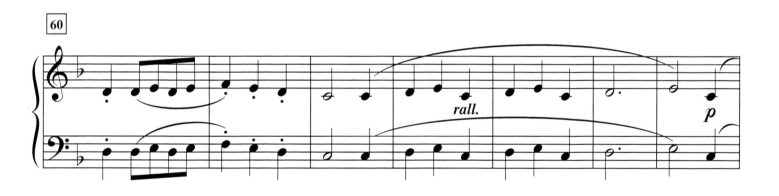

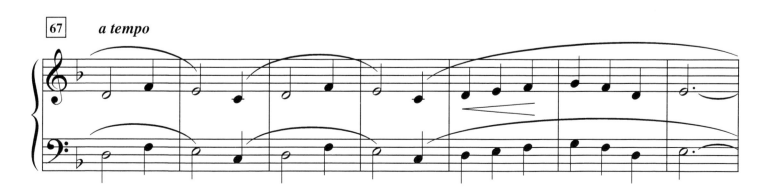

SECONDO (Teacher)

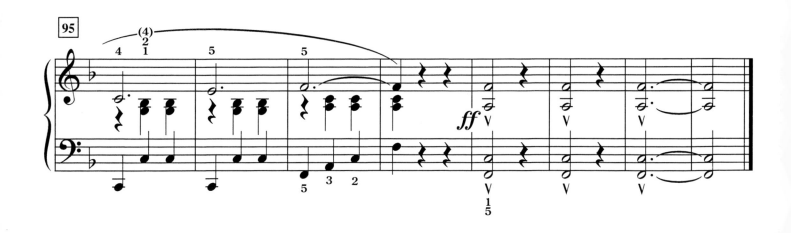

PRIMO (Student)

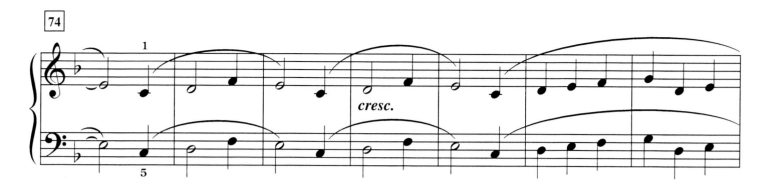

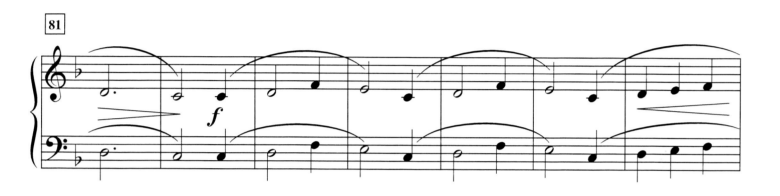

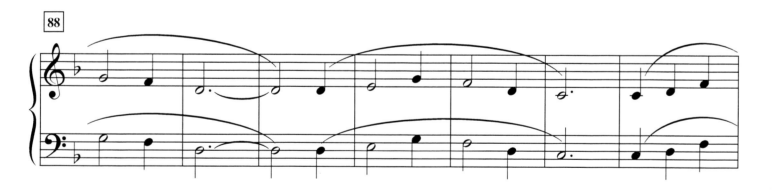

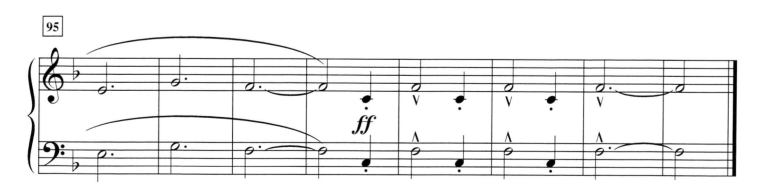

SECONDO
Teacher

The Wooden Horse
from *Illusions*

Albert Landry (dates unknown)
Op. 266, No. 1

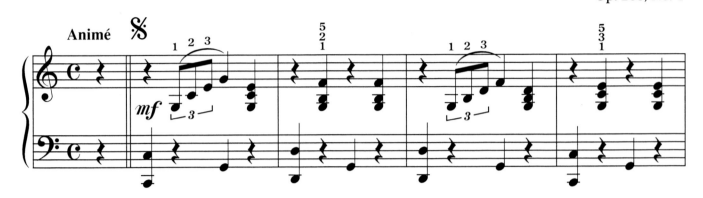

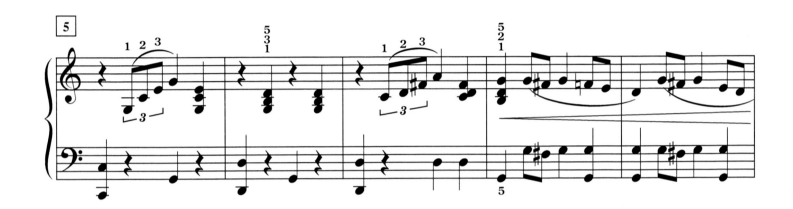

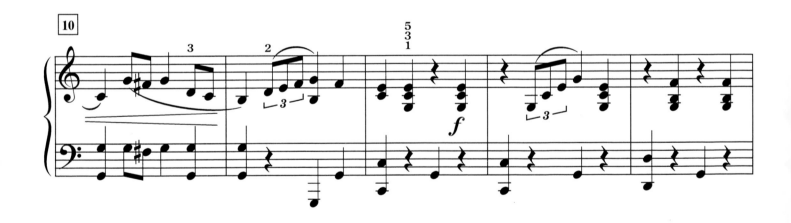

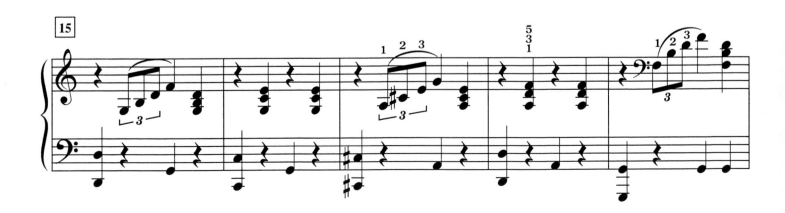

PRIMO
Student

The Wooden Horse

from *Illusions*

Albert Landry (dates unknown)
Op. 266, No. 1

Animé

Both hands two octaves higher than written throughout

SECONDO (Teacher)

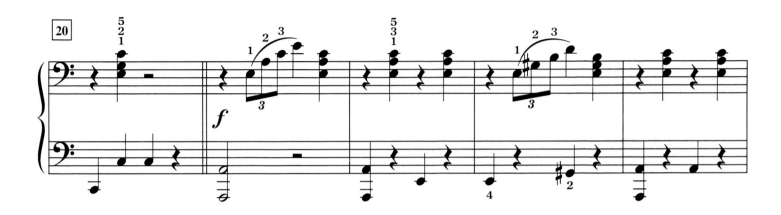

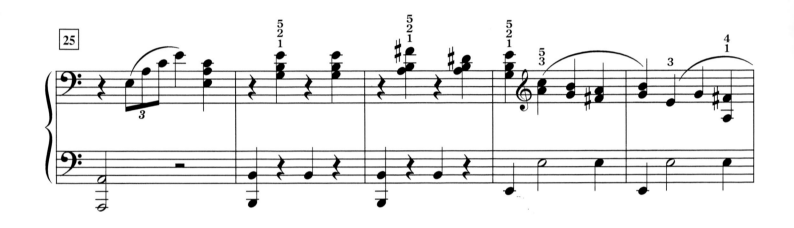

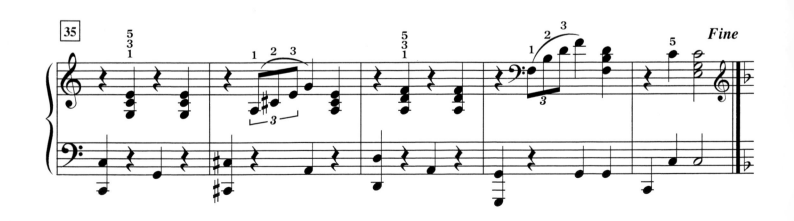

PRIMO (Student)

SECONDO (Teacher)

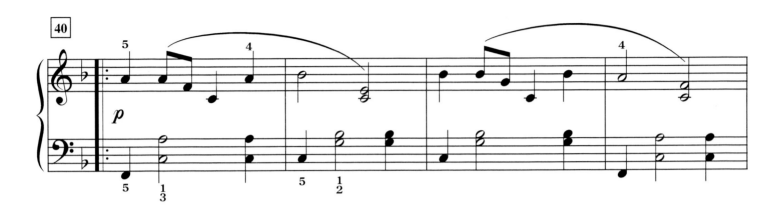

D. S. ℅ al Fine

PRIMO (Student)

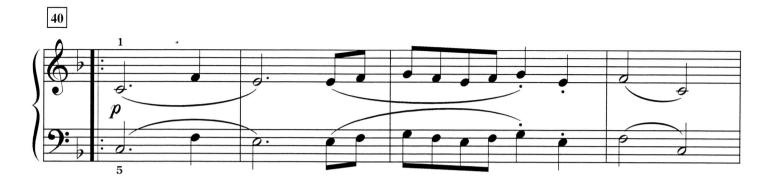

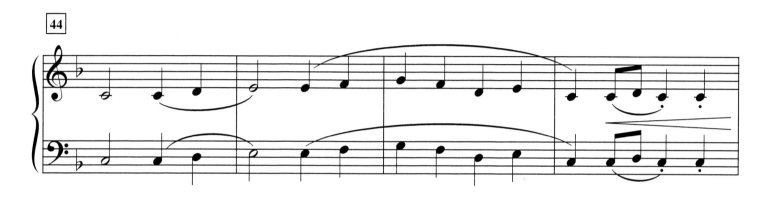

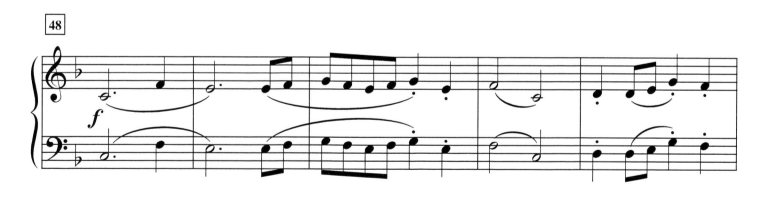

D. S. 𝄋 al Fine

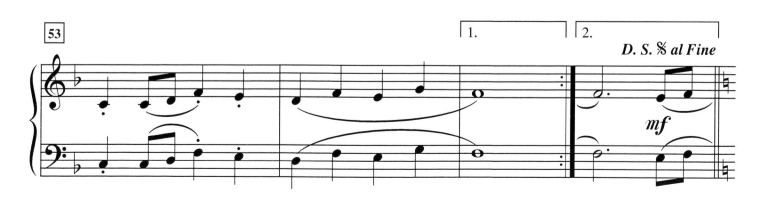

SECONDO
Teacher

Romanza
from *Melodious Pieces*

Anton Diabelli (1781–1858)
Op. 149, No. 11

PRIMO
Student

Romanza
from *Melodious Pieces*

Anton Diabelli (1781–1858)
Op. 149, No. 11

Andantino
Both hands one octave higher than written throughout

Andante
from *Vierhändige Clavierstücke*

Carl Reinecke (1824–1910)
Op. 54, No. 2

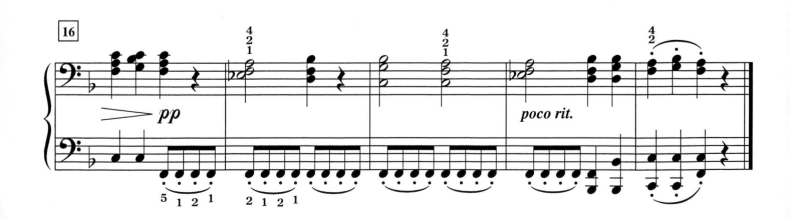

PRIMO
Student

Andante
from *Vierhändige Clavierstücke*

Carl Reinecke (1824–1910)
Op. 54, No. 2

Andante
Both hands two octaves higher than written throughout

SECONDO
Teacher

The Sleepy Boy
from *Ein Abend zu Hause*

Stephen A. Emery (1841–1891)
Op. 26, No. 6

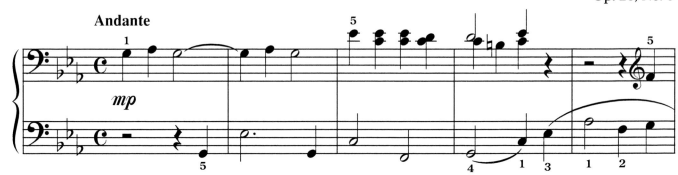

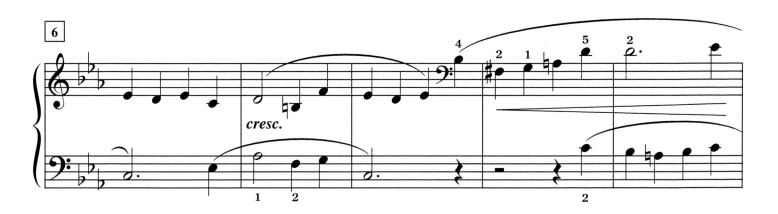

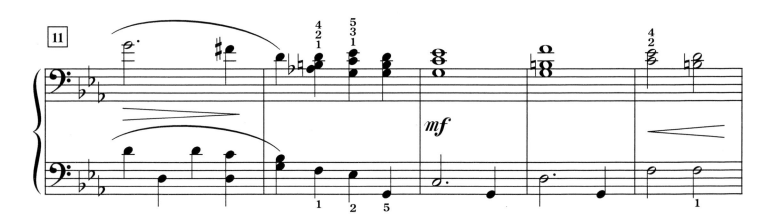

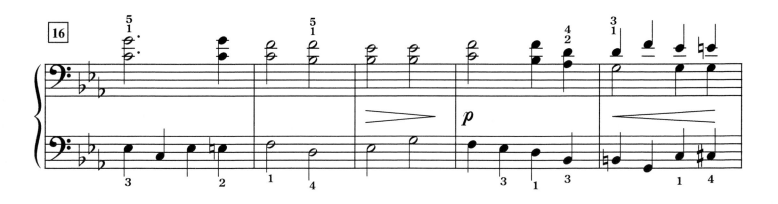

PRIMO
Student

The Sleepy Boy

from *Ein Abend zu Hause*

Stephen A. Emery (1841–1891)

Op. 26, No. 6

Andante   *Both hands one octave higher than written throughout*

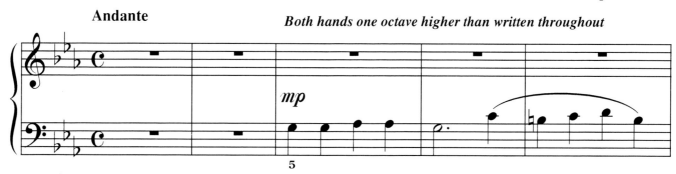

SECONDO (Teacher)

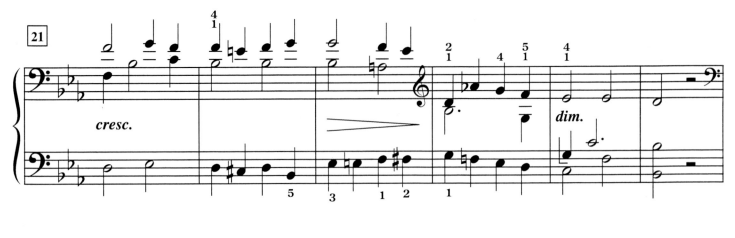

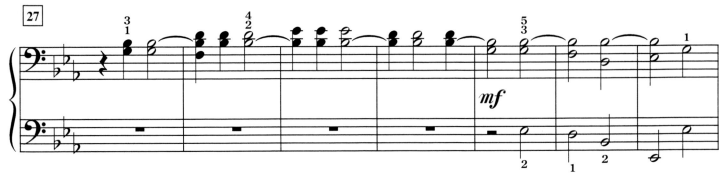

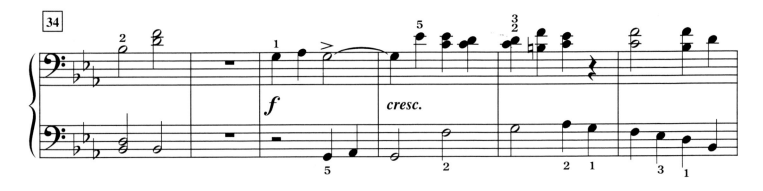

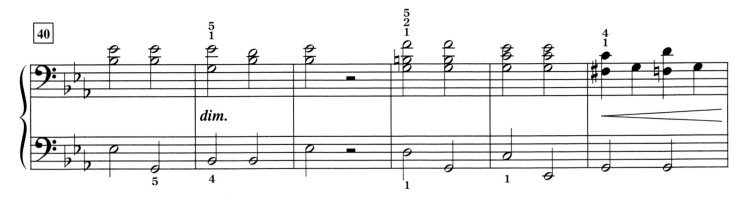

PRIMO (Student)

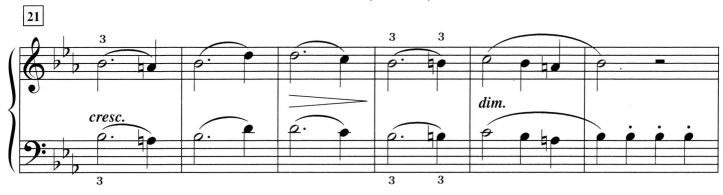

SECONDO
Teacher

The Bicycle
from *Illusions*

Albert Landry (dates unknown)
Op. 266, No. 3

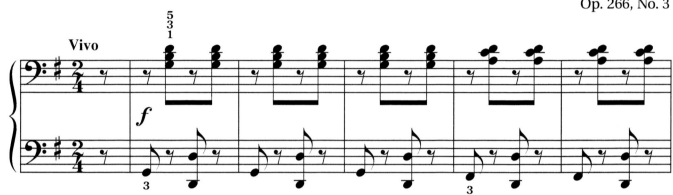

PRIMO
Student

The Bicycle
from *Illusions*

Albert Landry (dates unknown)
Op. 266, No. 3

SECONDO (Teacher)

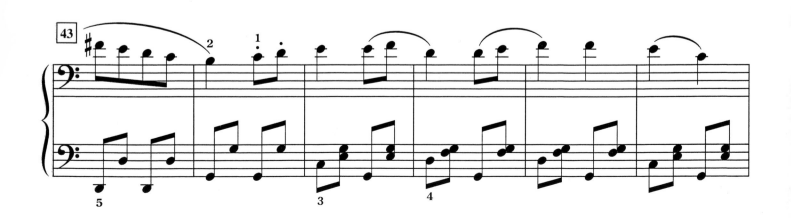

PRIMO (Student)

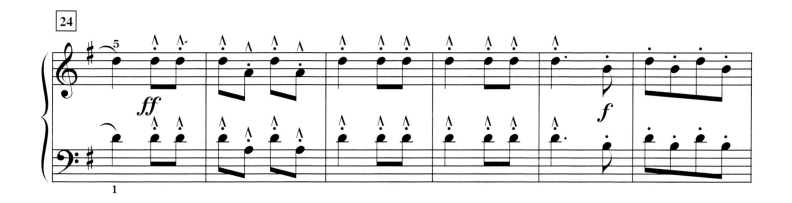

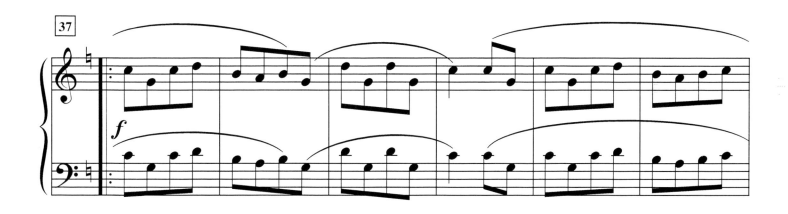

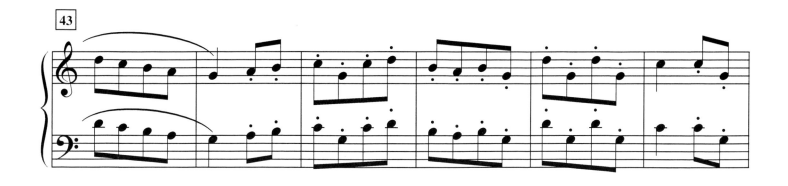

SECONDO (Teacher)

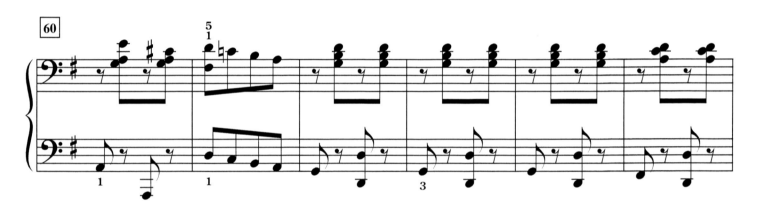

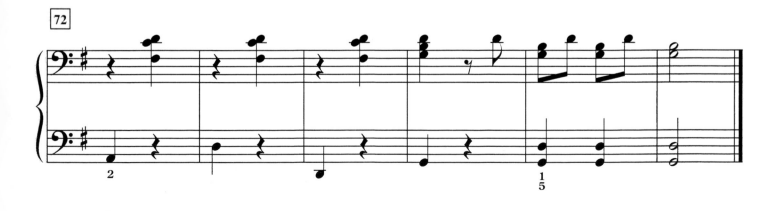

PRIMO (Student)

SECONDO
Teacher

Mazurka Amusante
from *Trois Morceaux*

François Grimaldi (dates unknown)
Op. 53, No. 2

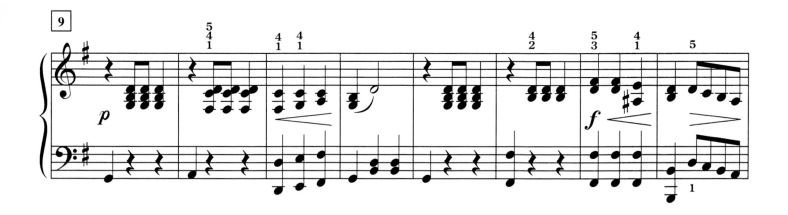

PRIMO
Student

Mazurka Amusante

from *Trois Morceaux*

François Grimaldi (dates unknown)
Op. 53, No. 2

Moderato
Both hands one octave higher than written throughout

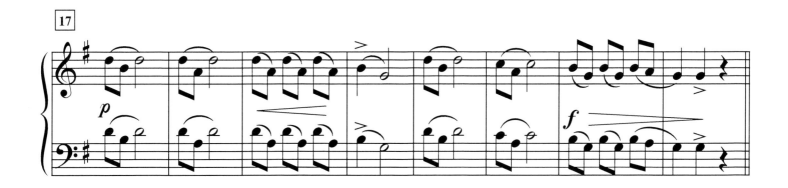

SECONDO (Teacher)

PRIMO (Student)

SECONDO
Teacher

Ballade
from *Leichte Compositionen*

Alois Rosenauer (dates unknown)
Op. 26, No. 1

Grave

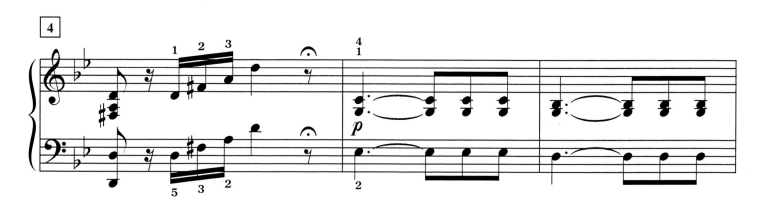

PRIMO
Student

Ballade
from *Leichte Compositionen*

Alois Rosenauer (dates unknown)
Op. 26, No. 1

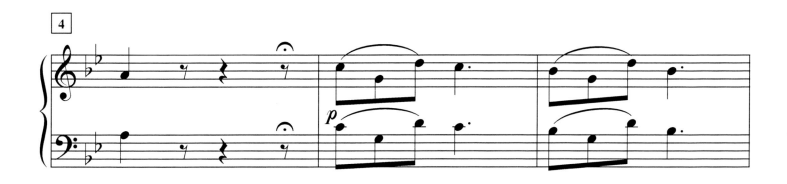

SECONDO (Teacher)

PRIMO (Student)

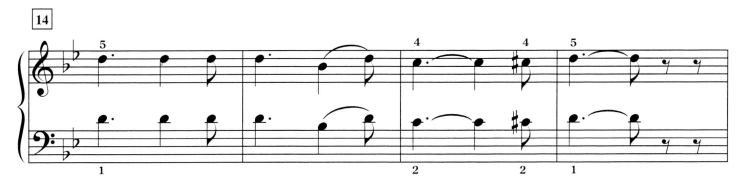

Allegro vivace

SECONDO (Teacher)

PRIMO (Student)

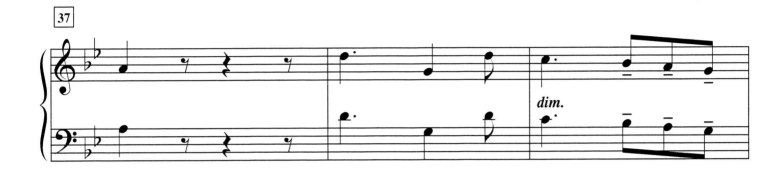

SECONDO
Teacher

Rondo
from *Pleasures of Youth*

Anton Diabelli (1781–1858)
Op. 163, No. 6

PRIMO
Student

Rondo
from *Pleasures of Youth*

Anton Diabelli (1781–1858)
Op. 163, No. 6

Allegro
Both hands two octaves higher than written throughout

52

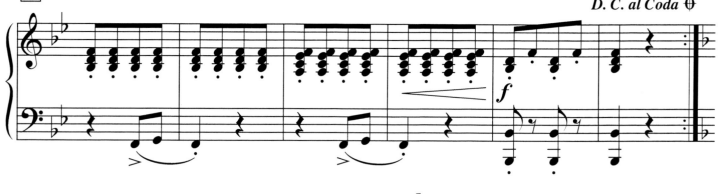

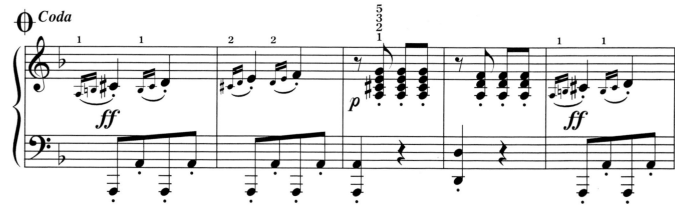

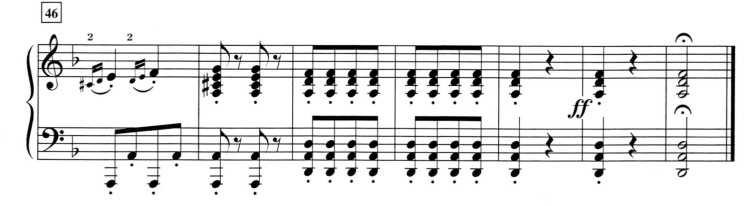

PRIMO (Student)

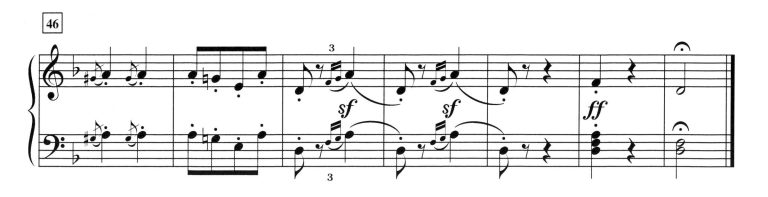

SECONDO
Teacher

Andante cantabile
from *Melodious Pieces*

Anton Diabelli (1781–1858)
Op. 149, No. 18

PRIMO
Student

Andante cantabile

from *Melodious Pieces*

Anton Diabelli (1781–1858)
Op. 149, No. 18

Andante cantabile
Both hands two octaves higher than written throughout

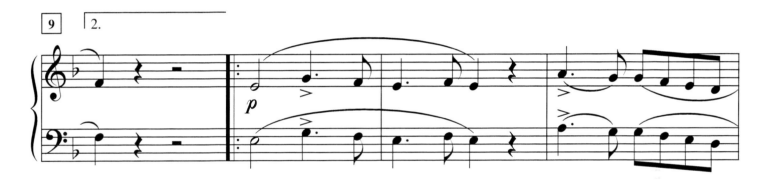

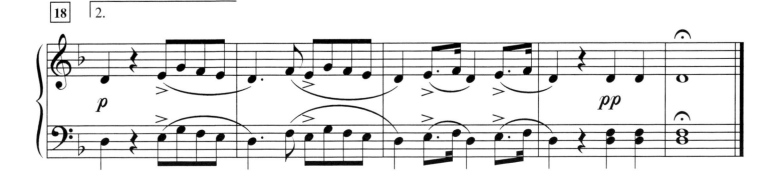

SECONDO
Teacher

Barcarole
from *Drei Vorspielstücke*

Alois Rosenauer (dates unknown)
Op. 17, No. 1

(not too slow)
Nicht zu langsam

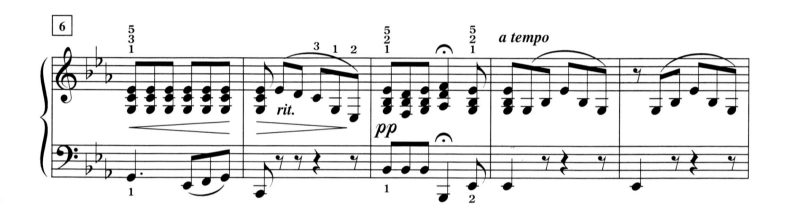

ⓐ The original meter is $\frac{12}{8}$. For ease in reading it has been changed to $\frac{6}{8}$.

PRIMO
Student

Barcarole

from *Drei Vorspielstücke*

Alois Rosenauer (dates unknown)
Op. 17, No. 1

(not too slow)
Nicht zu langsam

Both hands two octaves higher than written throughout

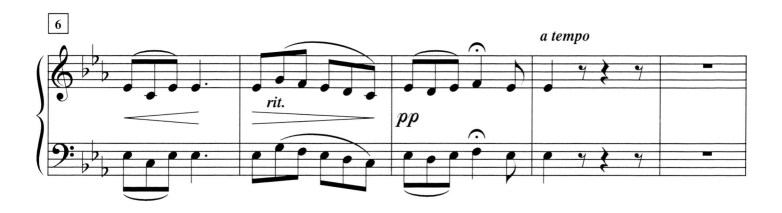

ⓐ The original meter is $\frac{12}{8}$. For ease in reading it has been changed to $\frac{6}{8}$.

SECONDO (Teacher)

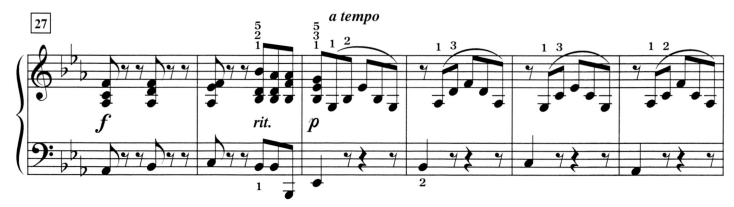

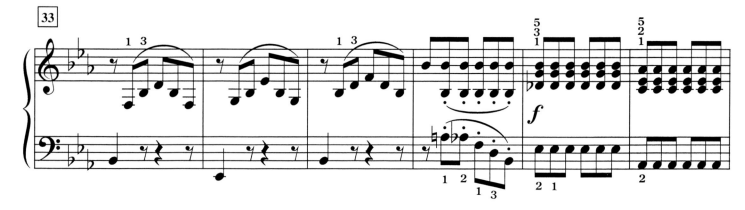

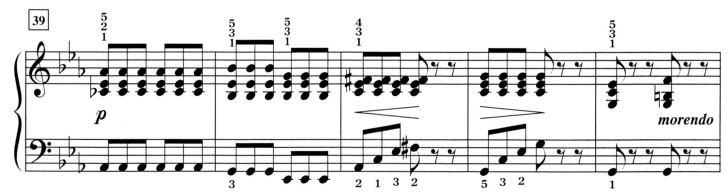

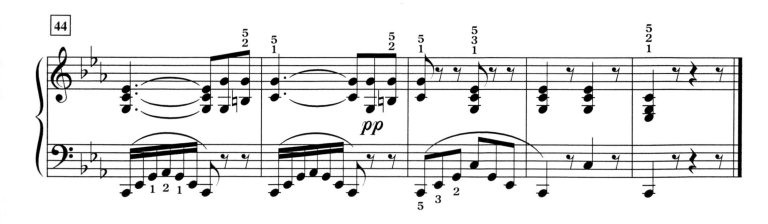

PRIMO (Student)

SECONDO
Teacher

Dance
from *Der Anfänger*

Cornelius Gurlitt (1820–1901)
Op. 211, No. 17

Allegretto scherzando

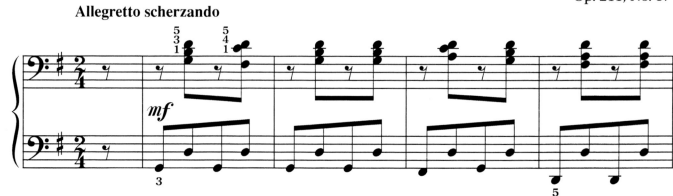

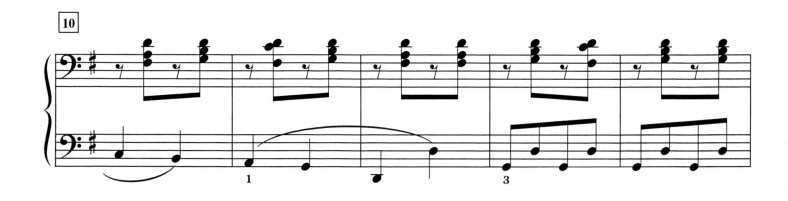

PRIMO
Student

Dance
from *Der Anfänger*

Cornelius Gurlitt (1820–1901)
Op. 211, No. 17

Allegretto scherzando
Both hands two octaves higher than written throughout

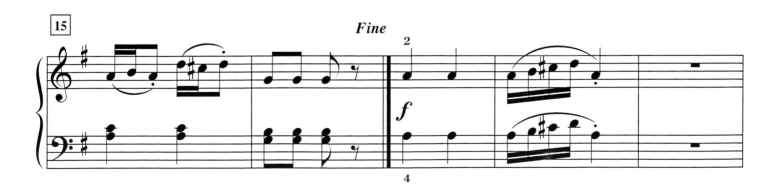

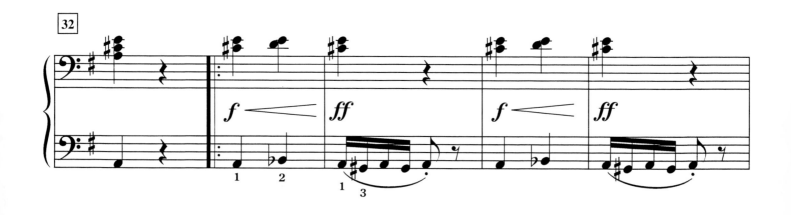

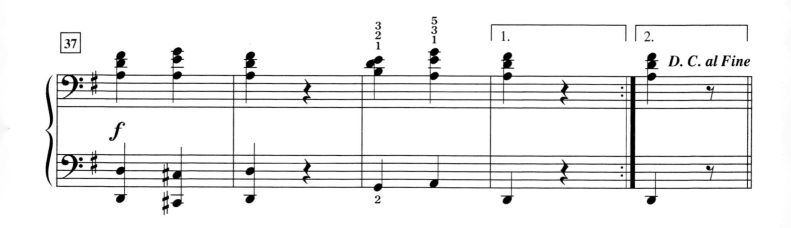

PRIMO (Student)

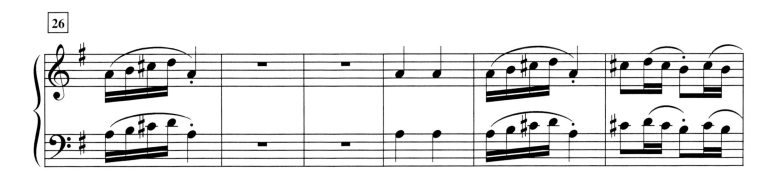

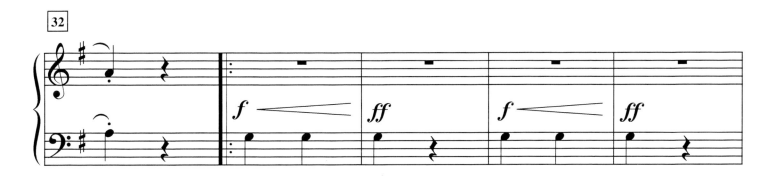

ABOUT THE COMPOSERS

Ernesto Becucci (1845–1905), an Italian, is best known for the light style and character of his piano works. He also wrote sacred music, songs and several sets of piano duets at the elementary and intermediate levels.

Anton Diabelli (1781–1858), an Austrian publisher and composer, wrote numerous piano duets. He was the publisher of Schubert's first printed works. An experienced musician, piano teacher and composer, he responded to the musical fashions of the time making his publishing company a huge financial success.

Stephen A. Emery (1841–1891), an American music teacher and composer, wrote textbooks as well as music. After study in Leipzig, he returned to the United States and taught at the New England Conservatory in Boston.

François Grimaldi (dates unknown) wrote several piano duets, many of which were published in both the United States and Leipzig in the late-19th century. Additional biographical information about him is unavailable.

Cornelius Gurlitt (1820–1901), a German, was a member of an artistic family. Active as an organist, he wrote operas and songs as well as numerous educational piano pieces. His piano miniatures are similar in style to the shorter works of Schumann. Among his piano works are several piano duets.

Albert Landry (dates unknown) wrote piano duets that were published in Paris in the early part of the 20th century. The students' parts of the duets contained in this collection were originally written as single lines on one staff. The student was instructed to play that line with the left hand and double it an octave higher with the right hand. Additional biographical information about him is unavailable.

Carl Reinecke (1824–1910) was a German pianist, conductor and prolific composer who authored several books. He taught both piano and composition at the Leipzig Conservatory. Known as an excellent performer of the works of Mozart, he traveled throughout Europe playing concerts.

Alois Rosenauer (dates unknown) wrote several collections of piano duets that were published in Germany in the early part of the 20th century. Additional biographical information about him is unavailable.